BY THOMAS K. ADAMSON

THE MINNESOTA
VIKINGS
STORY

BELLWETHER MEDIA · MINNEAPOLIS, MN

™

Are you ready to take it to the extreme? Torque books thrust you into the action-packed world of sports, vehicles, mystery, and adventure. These books may include dirt, smoke, fire, and chilling tales. **WARNING** : read at your own risk.

This edition first published in 2017 by Bellwether Media, Inc.

No part of this publication may be reproduced in whole or in part without written permission of the publisher. For information regarding permission, write to Bellwether Media, Inc., Attention: Permissions Department, 5357 Penn Avenue South, Minneapolis, MN 55419.

Library of Congress Cataloging-in-Publication Data

Names: Adamson, Thomas K., 1970-
Title: The Minnesota Vikings Story / by Thomas K. Adamson.
Description: Minneapolis, MN : Bellwether Media, Inc., 2017. | Series:
   Torque: NFL Teams | Includes bibliographical references and index.
Identifiers: LCCN 2015037694 | ISBN 9781626173729 (hardcover : alk. paper)
Subjects: LCSH: Minnesota Vikings (Football team)–History–Juvenile
   literature.
Classification: LCC GV956.M5 A33 2017 | DDC 796.332/6409776579–dc23
LC record available at http://lccn.loc.gov/2015037694TTTTT

Printed in the United States of America, North Mankato, MN.

TABLE OF CONTENTS

The Minnesota Vikings battle the Green Bay Packers for their 2015 division title. In the first half, both defenses play well.

Adrian Peterson

4

Teddy Bridgewater

The second half brings more scoring. Vikings **quarterback** Teddy Bridgewater hands off to **wide receiver** Adam Thielen. Thielen breaks free for 26 yards. **Running back** Adrian Peterson finishes the drive. Touchdown!

Everson Griffen

Soon after, **defensive end** Everson Griffen forces Green Bay to **fumble**. Minnesota recovers the ball for another touchdown!

The Packers cannot overcome Minnesota's lead. The Vikings beat their biggest **rival**. They also earn a home game for the **playoffs**!

SCORING TERMS

END ZONE

the area at each end of a football field; a team scores by entering the opponent's end zone with the football.

EXTRA POINT

a score that occurs when a kicker kicks the ball between the opponent's goal posts after a touchdown is scored; 1 point.

FIELD GOAL

a score that occurs when a kicker kicks the ball between the opponent's goal posts; 3 points.

SAFETY

a score that occurs when a player on offense is tackled behind his own goal line; 2 points for defense.

TOUCHDOWN

a score that occurs when a team crosses into its opponent's end zone with the football; 6 points.

TWO-POINT CONVERSION

a score that occurs when a team crosses into its opponent's end zone with the football after scoring a touchdown; 2 points.

The Vikings are a tough team. They are brave like the **Norsemen** they were named after. They fight hard in warm and cold weather.

Over the years, the team has collected
division and **conference** titles. They have
also made it to the **Super Bowl**. But their
fight for the top prize continues.

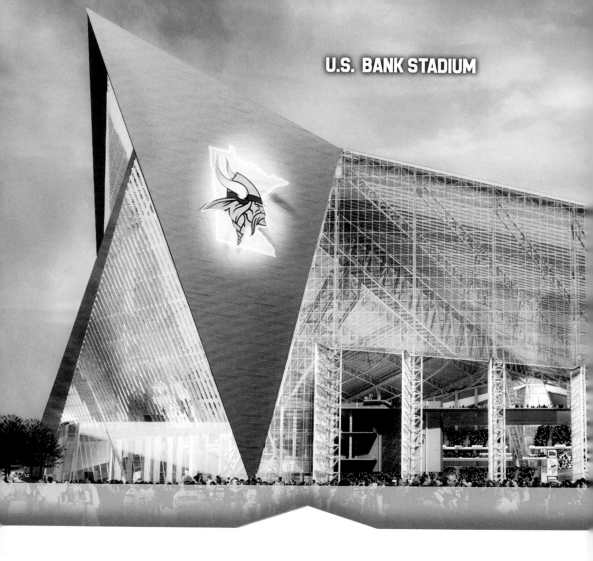

U.S. Bank Stadium is the Vikings' home in Minneapolis, Minnesota. Some fans think the stadium looks like a Viking ship.

Its see-through roof is made of a plastic-like material called ETFE. Sunlight can pass through it. The sloped roof is lightweight, but strong enough to support snow.

MINNEAPOLIS, MINNESOTA

OH NO, SNOW!

From 1982 to 2013, the Vikings played in the Metrodome. In 2010, heavy snow broke the roof.

W N E S

The Vikings play in the North Division of the National Football Conference (NFC). The other teams in the division are the Green Bay Packers, Chicago Bears, and Detroit Lions.

Games against the Packers are exciting border battles. Many Minnesotans cheered for the Packers before they had their own team.

NFL DIVISIONS

 **AFC**

AFC NORTH

 BALTIMORE **RAVENS**

 CINCINNATI **BENGALS**

 CLEVELAND **BROWNS**

 PITTSBURGH **STEELERS**

AFC EAST

BUFFALO **BILLS**

 MIAMI **DOLPHINS**

PATRIOTS

 NEW YORK **JETS**

AFC SOUTH

 TEXANS

 INDIANAPOLIS **COLTS**

 JACKSONVILLE **JAGUARS**

 TENNESSEE **TITANS**

AFC WEST

 DENVER **BRONCOS**

 CHIEFS

RAIDERS OAKLAND **RAIDERS**

 SAN DIEGO **CHARGERS**

NFC NORTH

 CHICAGO **BEARS**

 DETROIT **LIONS**

 GREEN BAY **PACKERS**

 MINNESOTA **VIKINGS**

NFC EAST

DALLAS **COWBOYS**

 GIANTS

 PHILADELPHIA **EAGLES**

 WASHINGTON **REDSKINS**

NFC SOUTH

 FALCONS

 CAROLINA **PANTHERS**

 NEW ORLEANS **SAINTS**

 BUCCANEERS

NFC WEST

 CARDINALS

 LOS ANGELES **RAMS**

 SAN FRANCISCO **49ERS**

SEATTLE **SEAHAWKS**

In 1961, the Vikings became the NFL's newest team. By the late 1960s, the Vikings had developed into a playoff team.

Bud Grant was behind the success. The strict coach led the Vikings for 18 seasons. He coached them to four Super Bowls.

SUPER BOWL 11
JANUARY 9, 1977

Bud Grant

More recently, the Vikings have had strong **offenses**. The 1998 team put up big scores and only lost one game all season. But the Atlanta Falcons beat the team in the NFC Championship game.

NFC CHAMPIONSHIP
JANUARY 17, 1999

In 2010, the Vikings lost another NFC
Championship. This time it was to the New
Orleans Saints.

VIKINGS
TIMELINE

1967

Traded quarterback Fran Tarkenton to the New York Giants; celebrated his return in 1972.

1961

Joined the NFL

1970

Won NFL Championship for the 1969 season, beating the Cleveland Browns (27-7)

1973

Won the NFC Championship, beating the Dallas Cowboys (27-10)

1967

Named Bud Grant as head coach

1970

Made their first Super Bowl appearance, but lost to the Kansas City Chiefs

7 FINAL SCORE **23**

1977

Made their fourth Super Bowl appearance, but lost to the Oakland Raiders

14 FINAL SCORE **32**

1974

Won the NFC Championship, beating the Los Angeles Rams (14-10)

2016

First played in U.S. Bank Stadium

1976

Won the NFC Championship, beating the Los Angeles Rams (24-13)

Fran Tarkenton was the Vikings' first star quarterback. He was also one of the NFL's first **mobile** quarterbacks. He scrambled to avoid being tackled.

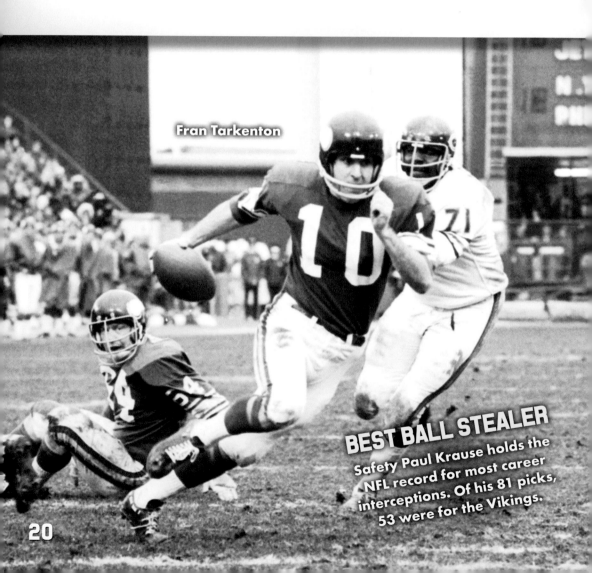

Fran Tarkenton

BEST BALL STEALER
Safety Paul Krause holds the NFL record for most career interceptions. Of his 81 picks, 53 were for the Vikings.

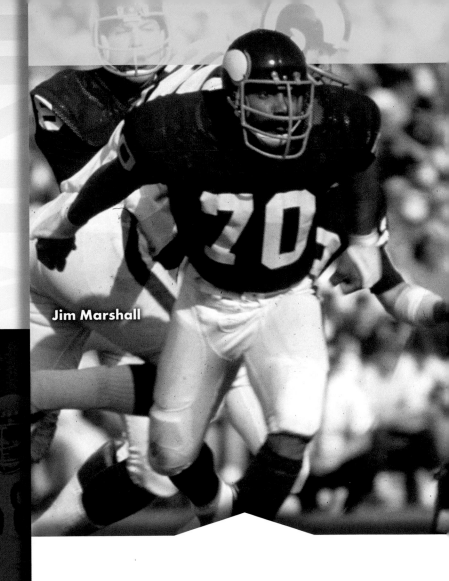

Jim Marshall

In the second half of his career, Tarkenton played with all-star **defensive linemen**. Alan Page, Carl Eller, Jim Marshall, and Gary Larsen were nicknamed the "Purple People Eaters."

Chuck Foreman was a powerful running back in the 1970s. He was hard to tackle and great at catching passes.

Bull-like Adrian Peterson now carries the ball. He led the NFL in **rushing yards** in the 2015 season. It was his third rushing title.

TEAM GREATS

FRAN TARKENTON
QUARTERBACK
1961-1966, 1972-1978

JIM MARSHALL
DEFENSIVE END
1961-1979

ALAN PAGE
DEFENSIVE TACKLE
1967-1978

TOUCHDOWN MACHINE

Wide receiver Cris Carter caught 110 touchdown passes as a Viking!

CHUCK FOREMAN
RUNNING BACK
1973-1979

CRIS CARTER
WIDE RECEIVER
1990-2001

ADRIAN PETERSON
RUNNING BACK
2007-PRESENT

Viking culture is everywhere at home games.
A large Viking horn sounds before kickoff. Its loud
blast announces that the Vikings are coming!

24

When the team scores, the fight song "Skol Vikings" plays in the stadium. *Skol* was a word Vikings yelled to encourage one another during battle.

Fans also dress like Viking warriors for games. Many wear "Helga hats." These hats feature large horns and long, yellow braids. The mascot, Viktor the Viking, even wears one!

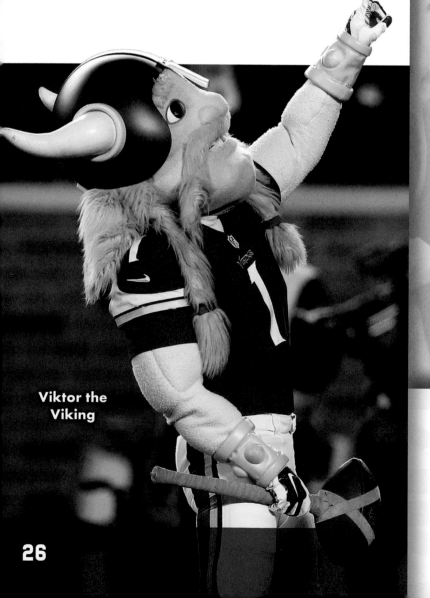

Viktor the Viking

The Purple and Gold have a lot of support from their home state!

MORE ABOUT THE
VIKINGS

Team name:
Minnesota Vikings

Team name explained:
**Named after fierce
warriors and the
Scandinavian heritage
of many Minnesotans**

Nicknames:
Vikes, Purple and Gold

Joined NFL: 1961

Conference: NFC

Division: North

**Main rivals: Green Bay Packers,
Chicago Bears**

Hometown:
Minneapolis, Minnesota

Training camp location:
Minnesota State University,
Mankato, Minnesota

MINNESOTA

MINNEAPOLIS

Home stadium name:
U.S. Bank Stadium

Stadium opened: 2016

Seats in stadium: 66,200

**Logo: A Norseman
with long gold hair, a
mustache, and a helmet
with horns**

Colors: Purple and gold

Mascot: Viktor the Viking

GLOSSARY

conference—a large grouping of sports teams that often play one another

defenses—groups of players who try to stop the opposing team from scoring

defensive end—a player on defense whose job is to tackle the player with the ball

defensive linemen—players on defense who try to stop the quarterback; defensive linemen crouch down in front of the ball.

division—a small grouping of sports teams that often play one another; usually there are several divisions of teams in a conference.

fumble—to lose the ball while it is still in play

mobile—able to move around easily

Norsemen—ancient people from the Scandinavian countries

offenses—groups of players who try to move down the field and score

playoffs—the games played after the regular NFL season is over; playoff games determine which teams play in the Super Bowl.

quarterback—a player on offense whose main job is to throw and hand off the ball

rival—a long-standing opponent

running back—a player on offense whose main job is to run with the ball

rushing yards—yards gained by running with the ball

Super Bowl—the championship game for the NFL

wide receiver—a player on offense whose main job is to catch passes from the quarterback

TO LEARN MORE

AT THE LIBRARY

Gilbert, Sara. *The Story of the Minnesota Vikings.* Mankato, Minn.: Creative Education, 2014.

Scarpati, Kevin. *Minnesota Vikings.* New York, N.Y.: AV2 by Weigl, 2015.

Schuh, Mari. *Adrian Peterson.* New York, N.Y.: Bearport Pub., 2013.

ON THE WEB

Learning more about the Minnesota Vikings is as easy as 1, 2, 3.

1. Go to www.factsurfer.com.

2. Enter "Minnesota Vikings" into the search box.

3. Click the "Surf" button and you will see a list of related web sites.

With factsurfer.com, finding more information is just a click away.

INDEX